Gifts from the Storm

HOW I CAME TO TRUST IN SPIRIT

Camila Abbot

Balboa Press books may be ordered through booksellers or by contacting:

Balboa Press
A Division of Hay House
1663 Liberty Drive
Bloomington, IN 47403
www.balboapress.com
1 (877) 407-4847

Cover artwork and all illustrations by Noelle Abbot

ISBN: 978-1-5043-4016-8 (sc)
ISBN: 978-1-5043-4017-5 (e)

Print information available on the last page.

Balboa Press rev. date: 11/2/2015

This work is a memoir which is to say that it reflects the author's interpretations and perceptions of the events described. Every effort has been made to protect the identities of those involved. To that effect, all names, places, timelines as well as any possibly identifying circumstances have been changed.

BALBOA.
PRESS
A DIVISION OF HAY HOUSE

PREFACE

In this work, the author shares the experience that changed her life forever. Eighteen years ago, she was a woman who felt trapped in an unhappy marriage and had lost touch with God or a Higher Power when, suddenly, her oldest child was diagnosed with cancer. His illness served as a catalyst for her to begin to examine her views on religion and spirituality, on the meaning and purpose of life, and on the difference between conditional versus unconditional love. It also led her to find work in a field where she could best utilize the lessons she had learned during her difficult journey. Most importantly, she was forever changed from being someone who did not trust in her intuition and was "deaf" to the voice of Spirit, to someone who began to listen to Its benevolent voice and who is now able to allow that guidance to lead her in life. So many years later, she finds that she has, finally, distilled the kernels of wisdom that were gifted to her, and she considers it her privilege to be able to share them with her readers.

To my beloved and most loyal supporter, L.B.P.

You know who you are…

To Ethan and Noelle - Constant bringers of joy

To Liam - My biggest teacher, my hero

Liam's Star

We emerge out from the stars,

And to the stars we will return

And I'll be up there shining bright,

Oh with great jubilee I'll burn,

And you might think I've left your side,

So loved, but silent as you dream

I'll be twinkling in the night,

A million miles above the ceiling,

And I'll be hoping when you see my star,

You'll smile to know I'm beaming.

Noelle Abbot

Chapter One

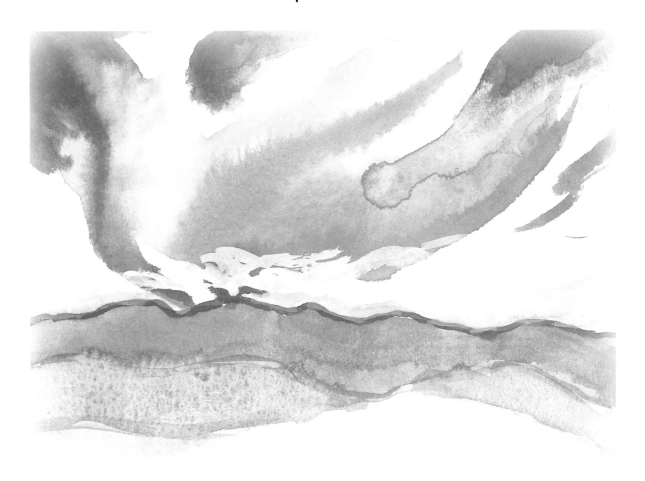

GATHERING WINDS...

End of the year 1996

There is no other way to say it, but to say it straight out. I was deeply unhappy. The best way to describe it is that I was in a constant state of confusion in regards to my husband. I had been married for ten years and I still did not feel that I knew him. He was a closed box-- more like a steel vault which was buried deep in the earth: unreachable to me. I had been knocking on that box for years, waiting for it to open, with no result.

I had been very naïve when I married my husband; I own up to the fact that I took everything he said to me as being true. I did not know yet that, when people open up to one another, more often than not, they share their own distorted views of who they are; unless they know themselves very well; unless they have taken the time to lead an examined life. I was eighteen years old when I met him and I had had no previous romantic experience before him. I didn't know then that everything he would say to me was something he chose to depict as the truth but it was not in fact true at all. The reality of the person he was and of the way he had grown up was something he could not face; therefore, he had created a better version-- the one he shared with me and with the rest of the world. I didn't realize then that, out of a desire to view everything and everyone in a positive light, I had also distorted and beautified my own version of my life before him. However, my version of the person I was, of how I wanted my life to be and of what mattered to me, was the real thing, the true thing and I shared that with him openly and transparently. You see, I had been examining my life up until I met my husband. I had spent a lot of time looking around me, at my family, the country I came from (New Zealand) and also at this new country which I had embraced at age thirteen. I had spent all that time, before him, observing, wondering about human nature and, especially, about relationships. I didn't see then that this particular thing, my fundamental need to lead an examined life versus his lack of need to do so would be the factor which would eventually pull us apart.

In the beginning, we got along fine but after three or four years, I began to notice a disassociation on his part; an indifference to my needs; a lack of caring to find out how I felt. A slow erosion in communication began to take place. We would have long conversations about matters that were very important to me and he would appear to listen and understand. We would agree to take certain steps to improve the relationship or how we parented our children and, then, he would not do anything to follow through with what had been mutually decided. It was very frustrating and I lived in a permanent state of confusion because with his words he would express agreement but with his actions, he would express non-agreement. I spent a lot of hours trying to make sense of his way of being; a way of existing that was utterly incomprehensible to me. I felt that if you are close to somebody, you can open your heart freely, you can say clearly how you feel and what you need and feel safe while doing so. His actions were telling me that he would not or could not be that open with me. It was as if he received some sort of satisfaction about getting his needs met or about expressing his real opinions in ways that, to me, felt underhanded. These incongruencies showed me that the differences between us were so large that they could split us apart, if something did not change.

Throughout our marriage, I had tried my best to communicate to him why I was so deeply unhappy; to talk from my heart to his heart with the hope of touching it. I finally had to conclude that, even though, on the whole, he was a good human being, generous and kind-hearted, he was not open to being known and, furthermore, was not interested in my love. I saw clearly that his actions were really inactions-- which to me communicated unlovingness, detachment and lack of caring. Possibly, it was not so much that he did not want to love but that he did not know how to love.

I had three young children: Liam, 8; Ethan, 6, and Noelle, 1. My day to day life was immersed in their caring. My husband was a busy financial consultant and I, previously a history teacher, had decided to stay home to care for them--with the long range plan of going back to school when the youngest entered kindergarten. However, by the summer of 1996, I had begun to entertain thoughts of divorcing my husband. I would describe myself as being inside a dark cave where my thought processes were continuously muddled and sad and where it was always cold and damp inside my mind. My thoughts ran like this: How can I do this to my children? … They did not ask to be raised in a world with a broken family… How am I going to survive as a single parent with no family around to help me?… Is it that I am the problem and I am asking too much of my husband?… We had been married for ten years by the end of 1996 and I did not want to throw all those years away but I was drowning in sorrow by the lack of attention and caring towards me, and was almost completely overwhelmed by the lack of help and involvement with the children and the household. The truth is that I was already functioning as a single parent, even though I was with him, but

I was still afraid; afraid to make a mistake that would potentially ruin my children's lives; afraid that it was selfish of me to divorce him because I was the only one suffering... The children were blissfully unaware of any issues; they were just happy being children and I worried that the repercussions of a divorce might be much more devastating on them.

During that period, I had stopped leading an examined life because I was spending so much time dealing with the confusion stemming from not understanding my husband and his actions. When there is no congruency between what someone says and what someone does, you know there must be something wrong. However, when you are blinded by the love you have already granted to someone, you don't want to believe that anything is wrong-- you want to believe that everything is right. That is what I had been doing for those ten years: struggling against the tide of truth which was slowly revealing itself to me in stronger and stronger currents, and together with raising my children, it took all the energy that I had in me. I was depleted physically, emotionally and spiritually. I was unhappy, I was heart-broken, I was desolate and inconsolable. I wanted love but I did not know yet what love is. I had been following the messages about love which had been given to me growing up; I had been expecting somebody else to make me happy rather than taking active steps to be happy with myself. I had not yet learned how to love myself... Did not even know what that would mean, what it would feel like, or what a difference it would make in my life if I did.

This was the state of mind I was in when, at the beginning of the year 1997, the bottom of my carefully self-contained world crumbled underneath me and I fell into a dark void...

And while in that void, I began to faintly hear the voice of Spirit...

Chapter Two

A STORM OF GRAY...

January 1997- December 1999

My husband and I had just moved into a new house, a few months before. To an outsider, we looked like a happy young couple with three adorable children. The reality was that there was no closeness, intimacy, honesty or respect present between us-- qualities that, in my opinion, are essential in a marriage. Without them, I felt that I could not be happy. I realized that we had failed to move in the same general direction of life. I was more and more intent on growing in authenticity and he was determined to stay the same. I saw crystal clear that I had "fallen in love" with the man I had imagined and wished to have in my life; that I had given those ideal attributes to my husband-- attributes he did not have but that he had subsumed during our courtship. When we first met, while attending college, in the Spring of 1984, I had been starved for companionship, for someone to talk to about life, about the deep parts of my soul, and with whom I could share my thoughts on relationships. In opening my heart to him and talking about all I cherished, I gave my husband (to be) a perfectly mapped route to my heart and he used that map very well-- if not consciously, then subconsciously-- to become in my eyes the perfect man for me to marry and have children with.

These realizations about the hollowness of my marriage were swirling around in my mind, when close to midnight on January 2, 1997, my husband and I were awoken by the cries of our son Liam-- who had just turned 9. We hurried to his bed as he said that he wasn't feeling well; I noticed that he was shaky as well. I took his temperature but he did not have a fever. Something did not feel right… We decided that I would stay home with the sleeping children and my husband would take Liam to the emergency room of the local hospital.

On the second floor of our house, there was an area with a balcony that looked out to a very large window and I spent four long hours sitting on the carpet as I looked out that window and waited for their return. Without explanation, I was sobbing uncontrollably the whole time-- as if something terrible had happened and I remember, wondering in the back of my mind, why I was crying but I just could not stop myself: the tears just ran and ran over my cheeks in an endless stream.

I see now that, at a deep level, I knew that something was seriously wrong with my son but how could I explain such knowledge? I had a very skeptical mind back then and it would never have occurred to me that there was an inner wisdom, available to me, informing me,

Those were the first whisperings of the voice of Spirit . . .

When several hours later, my husband and son returned from the emergency room, my swollen face greeted them and I was relieved to hear that Liam had been given a clean bill of health by the doctors; that they thought it was probably just a virus… and that they had done blood work –just in case. Half an hour later, just as we were getting ready to go to sleep, the phone rang and we were informed that the results of his blood work were abnormal and that we needed to take Liam to the Hematology/Oncology clinic first thing in the morning. There, after further testing, we were informed that our son had a cancer called neuroblastoma.

The bottom had just fallen out…

It is not my intention to chronicle in excruciating detail all the treatments and procedures Liam had to endure. Needless to say, it was extremely difficult, as a mother, to see him so ill and to not be able to protect him. What happened as a result of such a devastating situation was that, in the midst of my sad and confused world,

a window opened up… A window unto my soul, and through it, Spirit began to speak…

It began to speak to me in ways which I had ignored in the past but which I could no longer ignore because of its magnifying intensity, and because of the tumultuous situation I was now experiencing.

The first area that began to shift within me was my view on religion. Growing up in New Zealand, I had been raised as a Catholic but I was not devout. Throughout the years, I had come to feel discontented with many of the beliefs that had been instilled in me and which no longer made sense. After Liam was diagnosed, my discontent only grew. I noticed that the comments made by the clergy felt empty and did not resonate with me. Comments such as: "The Lord does not send you a burden heavier than you can carry" were very often said to me. Questions such as: "Aren't you angry at God"or "Aren't you asking yourself, why me?" were not helpful to me either.

What I came to realize on my own, during the first months after Liam's diagnosis, was that I could not believe in a God or a Higher Power that would reach out from the heavens, point to my dear child and give him cancer; that was unimaginable to me. What I did find myself asking was:"Why not me?" I saw that I had been living my life, thinking that, as long as I was a good person, somehow God would protect me and my family. I truly saw then that, in my mind, I had been thinking that awful things like cancer only happened to other people but would never happen to me or to my loved ones because we were protected. It was shocking and horrifying for me to see just how deluded I had been!

Spirit whisper: The loving force we call God loves all of us unconditionally and bad things are not sent to us by It. The truth about life is that, at any moment, bad things can happen to anyone. Human beings are like little gnats, happily flying around under the illusion that they are never going to die, when in truth, at any given moment, the windshield of the car of life can hit them and they are gone! That notion is too hard for humans to accept; it makes them feel too fearful…

On January 2, 1997, I was presented with that truth. Spirit placed it in front of me and it was up to me to either face it and grow or evade it and shrink spiritually. I chose to face it.

As I was grappling with the spiritual questions arising from my son's illness, and the challenges and physical demands of every day, I knew that some things would have to be put aside for later-- including the one main issue that had been entirely occupying my thoughts before he became sick. Once Liam was diagnosed, there was no question of getting a divorce. If I knew anything, I knew that I could not in any way add to his distress by separating him or my other children from their father at this time. And Liam adored his father…

Spirit whisper: Do not worry, my child. I will let you know when the time is right to take action regarding your marriage. This is not the time

Ethan was 8 years old and Noelle was 3 years old when Liam was diagnosed (at age 9) so I was a very busy mother with the additional doctor and hospital appointments for Liam. Amidst the whirlwind of all this activity, I was always thinking about what all of this meant. Having been shaken out of my complacent and false sense of security by my son's illness, I began to feel terrified whenever one of my other children showed the smallest sign of illness. I wanted them to have blood tests-- to rule out cancer-- and experienced tremendous amounts of anxiety, until one day I heard the following…

Spirit whisper: You must let go of any fears, my child. I am with you and you need to relax into my arms and trust that you will be able to face anything that may come your way, even if that includes a serious illness for one of your other children. Know that I am with you always. Lean on me…

After I let go of the tight grip the fear for my other children had over me, a peace filled my soul that is still with me to this day and that I cherish as one of the gifts that came with this storm.

Spirit whisper: Human beings are not in control of some of the random and tragic events in their lives and neither is God. However, they are in control of how they respond to those events

I chose not to blame the loving presence of God for what Liam and my family were going through. Instead, I leaned on Its peaceful love in order to continue to function and to survive. During this time, I used to see, in my mind's eye, a loving presence, with tears in Its eyes, looking at me and my son and I felt that It was going through this together with us.

I also realized that I had been trying to take care of my problems all on my own and would only think of asking for God's guidance as a last resort. I saw that I needed to reverse that order.

Spirit whisper: Call on me at the onset of a problem and I will lead you in the right direction, will put the right people in your path to help you and will support you throughout. Know that I cannot help you unless you ask…

I clearly remember feeling so powerless to help my son. Mothers are supposed to help their children, and every step of the way, I felt that there must be more I could do for him … After receiving the bad news that Liam had relapsed (5 months into the treatment course), I told him: "I would give anything to trade places with you, so that I would have all the treatments and you would be spared!" He just looked at me silently, his eyes conveying that he knew that I meant it wholeheartedly and that he truly felt my love for him.

There were many drives to the hospital for Liam to receive treatments (a one and a half hour trip) during which I would be immersed in my thoughts: fearful, angry, sad thoughts… when, all of the sudden, some unseen force would make me turn to look at Liam-- sitting on the passenger's seat-- only to realize that he had already been looking at me. Those old soul eyes of his which always communicated to me that he knew what I was going through. It was an uncanny experience; to look at my child's eyes and get in touch with the fact that I was looking at a wise and old spirit, inside the body of an innocent child.

Spirit whisper: You have been pondering about what love is. It is time for you to realize that the love children offer parents is completely unconditional; while what you have thought to be love thus far, has been conditional love. The love your parents, relatives and friends have offered you has come with conditions. Even the love you have offered your husband has come with conditions. It is time for you to see that true love can only be unconditional

In July of 1999, after two and a half years of grueling treatments, my husband and I met with Liam's oncologist and were informed that Liam had six months or less to live. All the treatments had been unsuccessful and there were no other options available to him. How can a parent survive after hearing those words? The way I did it was by going on automatic pilot; I had to, in order to continue to care for my children and in order to help Liam live fully until it was his time to leave us and this world. We took him to the beach and he had a marvelous time with his father and brother; watching a school of dolphins jump high out of the water right in front of him; looking for sand crabs and shells with his family. He played in the sun and sand and was able to feel normal, and to be relaxed and joyful. He reconnected with what it is like to be a natural, carefree child. What a blessing that trip was to him and to those around him!

During those years, I held long conversations with God about how difficult it was to live with someone I no longer loved and the answer I received, every time, was a resounding silence. Until one night, about one month after Liam relapsed, when I heard this…

Spirit whisper: It is time for you to separate from your husband until the time is right to divorce

The only way I can explain it is that I felt an unshakeable sense of knowing that that was the next step to take. And as scary as it was, I decided to listen to Spirit. I was beginning to learn to trust in It.

I simply felt that if I did not separate from my husband, I would die. This is not an exaggeration. The physical impossibility of continuing in the marriage struck me most fully because I was deeply aching emotionally and spiritually. The act of preparing myself for my son's impending death was crushing my heart, while, at the same time, it was opening my eyes to a deeper knowingness about love, about what this life is for, about religion and spirituality, and about the true state of my relationships with family and friends. I had been going through the process of my son's illness and had come to realize the briefness of life and had become connected to the fountain of unconditional love inside of him and that had changed things for me. With my awareness expanding in new directions, the path towards living a more authentic life was being illuminated for me and I was ready to take the steps onwards into its light. To be, at the same time, maintaining a false front of a marriage, for the sake of our children, became a less and less worthwhile way to spend my brief time upon this earth. I knew that I had to model for my children the importance of truly living life while you have it. I had reached the point where it was not survivable for me to continue with my husband.

Spirit whisper: It is not selfish to take active steps to be true to yourself. You are being self-loving when you do that. If you stay in the marriage, your children would eventually see that you no longer love or respect your husband and that would be highly detrimental to them. The best gift you can give to your children is to grant yourself the permission to be happy and to continue to grow in authenticity and self-awareness.

Once I made the decision to separate from my husband, I did not expect the lack of support I experienced from some family members and friends. Practically everyone, it seemed, felt that what mattered the most was for me to be financially secure and because I had stayed at home with my children they feared for me and told me, in no uncertain terms, that I should stay with my husband. What nobody realized was that there is nothing like having one's child face a terminal illness to push a person towards a great transformation; to make someone question what really matters in life and because of it, I was a changed woman. Before Liam's diagnosis, I had never cared much about the material things in life but I had enjoyed having them. Later on, it became clear to me that the only things that matter are love and truth; because when you live from the commitment to grow in love and to be truthful, you are able to experience real inner peace.

My husband and I separated while living in the same house; I chose to move into the guest room while he stayed in the master bedroom. This took place in August of 1999. At about that time, Liam began to show an intense interest in the weather and the skies; he would watch the Weather channel and had books on the weather. It is as if his subconscious knew that he was going to die and he, as a child, equated that better place with the skies. He was fascinated whenever he saw "God's light"-- those beautiful sheets of rays of light that filter down from the clouds-- and when he saw rainbows appearing after a storm. He also began to wear two watches, one on each wrist. I noticed this habit and thought it was strange but did not dwell on it at the time. Only later, did I realize that the subconscious message he was receiving was: Time is running out. Another thing he did that was out of the ordinary, in those months, was to write his and his siblings' letters to Santa at the beginning of September. You think I should have realized then that, at some level, probably subconsciously, he must have known that he was not going to be alive at Christmas time but I did not make that connection at all. I could not see because I did not want to allow myself to have even the smallest thought that Liam may die; even after hearing the doctor say that he had six months or less left here on this earth.

Spirit whisper: *The actions of young children are driven by the subconscious. If you had asked Liam why he was doing such things; he would not have been able to tell you. It is up to the adults to see what their children's actions are telling them…*

"But how can a parent ever see those signs when he or she cannot imagine life without their child?"

Liam went into the hospital for the last time on the night of December 2, 1999 and he stayed there for 14 days. On the night of December 15, I was in bed with Liam thinking how sad it was that I would not be in heaven or in the space our spirits go after we die and would not be able to receive him after he died when, all of the sudden, I smelled the sweetest, most wonderful essence; it pervaded the entire space: it was not in Liam's hospital blanket or in his clothes or in mine; it seemed not to be a part of any of the objects in the room, but rather, to be diffused into the space between us… That essence made me think of the scent of white roses. I shook my head and found it to be odd but I was focusing on other things, such as the fact that my son was getting worse…

I had been with Liam every moment of every day he had been in the hospital and I was feeling tired: physically and emotionally. The following day, December 16, one of the nurses came into the room and asked my husband and me to go with her to the nurses' station. Without saying a word, we complied. Sadly, he took his last breath while we were away…

Chapter Three

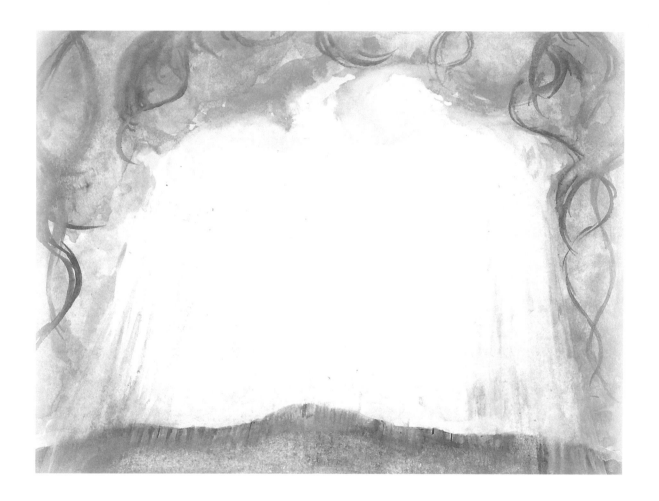

RAYS OF LIGHT FILTERING THROUGH THE CLOUDS...

December 1999-Present

When Liam died on December 16, a part of me died with him. But right away, I began to receive signs from him. After his funeral, as we were driving back to our house, the skies opened up and the widest array of God's light filled the expanse of sky. We all smiled and took it to mean that he was letting us know that he was ok. It would take years for me to remember about the strong scent of roses as he was dying but, later on, when I did allow that awareness into my consciousness, I heard the following...

Spirit whisper: I know that you are sad because you were not there to welcome your child but know that a loving presence (hence the sweet scent of roses) was waiting to receive him. I know that is not what you wished but things do not always go the way humans want them to. Trust in me...

One year after Liam's death, I divorced my husband. Even though, I had been raised as a Catholic and had carried that Catholic guilt ingrained in my consciousness ever since childhood, I knew, deep in my soul, that it was the right thing to do, and that superseded any fears I had had about it. How did I know for sure that this was the right decision? By the deep sense of peace I felt afterwards...

Going through a divorce while grieving the death of a child is a very difficult thing. My children and I went through a very long period of adjustment due to all the changes and the sadness that came with not having Liam with us.

Both children, of course, really missed their big brother. My son, Ethan, was ten years old when his brother died and Noelle had just turned five. Ethan did not talk about his sadness, however, and seemed to keep it more inside. I took him to a grief counselor early on in order to make sure he received the support he needed. Noelle, on the other hand, talked about Liam all the time. To her, he was ever-present in her games, drawings and everyday life. I could not allow myself to grieve until I had first helped my children adjust, but once I felt we had at least a semi-solid footing in our new surroundings, I started seeking an outlet of my own. A year after his death, I went to a grief counselor myself and found it to be such a relief to be able to talk non-stop about my son. Friends and family did not allow me to do that; they tried to spare my emotions by avoiding the subject-- which only made me feel more alone than ever. They did not see that I needed to validate the fact that Liam had existed, that he had mattered and that he had left a mark in all of our lives.

I was thirty three years old and felt like an empty vessel. I felt that life was not worth living after Liam died and were it not for Ethan and Noelle, I think I would have given up on life completely. I felt as sad as it is humanly possible to feel.

I was angry, but not so much about Liam's death; my views about what we are here in this world for and about death had expanded to encompass the fact that his death was not anybody's fault and that he had come to teach me, to teach us all, about what it means to love. No, what I was most angry about was the realization that my own life had not turned out the way I had envisioned it. I had married for life and never thought I would ever divorce but I had to learn that it truly takes two people to keep a marriage alive.

Spirit whisper: *My beloved child, you, like all human beings, are here to grow spiritually and to let go of the need to control everything that happens in your life. You are all here to surrender and to get out of your own way so that you can live lives filled with abundance, joy and happiness and to be instruments to help others do the same. And the loving bond you have with those you care about is eternal and continues after death. I know you miss Liam but know that he is still around you, loving you!*

A few weeks after he died, I began to have vivid dreams about Liam. In all of them, he would tell me how much he loved me and hug me tightly. I would wake up and think: This felt more like a visit than a dream. I could actually feel his arms encircling me.

One night, I was deep in sleep and was dreaming of Liam, when all of the sudden, Ethan came into the room and interrupted my "dream"… At that moment, I felt a part of me come back into my body. It was surprising and abrupt. I had read books that described the existence of the astral body-- a spiritual, etheric counterpart to the physical body-- but I had not really believed in such a thing. However, like another clue in piecing together the connection between the living and the afterlife, after that experience, I became wholly convinced that there is an astral body that leaves our physical bodies while we are asleep and visits other realms. How else could I have explained that abrupt sensation of myself returning back into myself? That new awareness explained to me why if I had been struggling with an issue, sometimes after sleeping, I would wake up with a sense of renewed confidence and peace-- as if I had received wisdom and guidance from above.

Far from scaring me, these experiences gave me an incredible sense of peace and reassurance that we are not alone in life; that we have many sources of guidance and support from other realms and dimensions which are unseen to most but which indeed exist. The skeptical woman who only believed in what she could see had changed indeed!

Liam continued to send me signs from the other side-- connections with things he had loved while he was alive, which he sent into my path now that he was no longer with us in body. The most treasured example of this phenomenon came to me in quite an unexpected way. Back in the Winter of the year 1996, a few months before Liam was diagnosed, I had taken the children to the theater to watch the movie "An American Tail." A few months later, as I was driving down the road, with kids in tow, I was listening to the radio when the theme song from that same movie started playing: "Somewhere out there" with Linda Ronstadt singing… From the backseat, I heard Liam pipe in: "Mama, that's our song!" I could see his big, dimpled smile in the rearview mirror. It touched me so much that he had picked a song that expressed his feelings for me… and it was a song that comforted the listener with words of love!

I had no way of knowing, at that time, how this small moment would comfort me years later, and help me feel connected with him for the rest of my life. A few days before Christmas of the year 1999, only a few days after Liam's death, I was walking, absentmindedly and numbingly, about the aisles of a shopping mall store when I felt drawn to a small box with a lacquered top showing a little boy-- sitting on a crescent moon with a paintbrush on his hand-- painting a yellow star on a dark blue sky. Noticing the little boy induced me to pick up the box and noticing that it was a music box, I turned it over to find out that the song it played was: "Somewhere out there". I knew then that Liam had just picked out his Christmas gift for me and was letting me know of his presence in our lives… and he did so in ways that were very clear to me, particularly in the first few months after his death.

A few days later, in the early morning of Christmas Day that year, around 5:00 or 5:30 am, as all of us were deep in sleep, I was awakened by the sound of fast and loud steps going down the stairs to our living room where the Christmas tree was with all the presents. The steps ran down and then up and then down again several times and there was no doubt that they were real. I felt then that Liam was still with us and I was comforted…

Because of these incidents, I was not surprised when, on the first anniversary of Liam's death, as I was driving to the cemetery with Ethan and Noelle and turned on the radio, the song: "Somewhere out there!" started playing …I got goose bumps and knew for certain that Liam was letting us know that he was with us!

Spirit whisper: *Whenever you get goose bumps, trust that Spirit is speaking to you; that you are in touch with an unshakeable truth*

For a long time afterwards, I continued to feel angry as well as deeply sad about life; I felt disappointed about how the marriage had turned out and I also tortured myself with feelings of guilt and regret about not having been perfect for my son all the time. I would remember trivial things such as Liam asking me to go upstairs to watch him play a certain game and me telling him that I needed to finish washing the dishes, and I would cry bitter tears about not always having dropped everything for him; about not being perfect. It has taken a lot of years for me to come to terms with the fact that for every time I did not do something right, there were a hundred times I did but I had chosen to dwell on the one time and to forget about the other hundred.

Liam came to be my biggest helper in aiding me to understand that… With his spirit, he sought beautiful ways to tell me to forget about the unnecessary details and to focus only on the most important things: the love we had shared together and our special bond which would never die. I would also get affirmations of his presence in my life through animals and objects that were beloved by him, while he was alive.

He loved cardinals, butterflies, especially monarch butterflies and feathers (he had a collection). When I was feeling particularly down, I would receive some sort of sign such as the brightest red cardinal flying just in front of me or a butterfly alighting near me or a feather would materialize in the most unlikely place (such as in the middle of a busy airport). And I would feel my heart get a little lighter because I knew that Liam was still around.

Spirit whisper: Listen to your child. He is letting you know that what matters is love. He felt loved by you and he needs for you to feel loved by him. Stop torturing yourself by dwelling on minutiae

I also struggled with the feeling that I had let Liam down because I was not with him, holding his hand, when he died.

Spirit whisper: People choose who is going to be present when they die and, oftentimes, children have difficulty dying in front of their parents, because they are protective of them until the very end

Three years after Liam's death, I had assimilated the fact that I had learned many lessons about what parents, children who are terminally ill and their siblings feel and need in their journey and decided to go back to school to pursue a master's degree. I began with a few courses on Family Studies, but after my first semester, I was introduced to a social worker at the university hospital who said to me: You need to become a social worker. My reaction was: "What is a social worker?" I had never heard of it and dismissed his advice but I did not forget it. A few months later, I looked up a description of the social work degree and realized that it matched perfectly what I wanted to do.

Spirit whisper: Do not be so stubborn, my child. I am putting people in your path to guide you towards what you can do with the lessons you have learned and you dismiss them outright. I am glad you decided to finally listen…

In the Fall of 2002, I enrolled in a two year master's degree program for Social Work. It was difficult, psychologically, to go back to school after staying at home for so many years. However, I found that if the younger students were faster in their thinking and test-taking abilities, I surpassed them in wisdom and patience, and that realization helped boost my confidence level.

It was a requirement to do a year and a half of practicum/internship at a place of work that interested the student; so I decided to sign up for my first practicum at the local Children's hospital; in the Pediatric Oncology unit. It brought back painful memories for me... It also got me in touch with the realization that, in the hospital setting, there seemed to be a disconnect with feelings. While children were being treated for life-threatening illnesses, the doctors and nurses did their best to try to stay positive and to make the waiting area and treatment rooms as inviting and non-threatening as possible, but nobody seemed to notice the deep sadness and fear in the parents' eyes. Just like it was for me, nobody was addressing the grief the parents were experiencing. It used to frustrate me; it felt unfair that I had to reach deep within my depleted state to offer understanding to the very medical personnel who were treating my child and other children and who were supposed to be the experts.

Spirit whisper: Do not become embittered or disheartened. The medical personnel are caring people who cannot do everything. They have to deal with children who might die and it is very hard for them to put their hearts on the line all the time. Ideally, there would be a special team at hospitals which would be available to provide support and counseling to parents, children and siblings from the time of diagnosis and onwards

During this first practicum, I realized that the lessons I had learned through my experience with Liam would be better suited for a different setting. Someone mentioned to me the word hospice. I had never before heard of hospice and was intrigued. I found out that one of the hospices in our town had a pediatric program and when I met with the director of the program, she turned out to be a very smart, compassionate and caring young woman. She accepted my request for a year-long practicum and I was elated.

That practicum changed my life. I realized right away that I felt at home at hospice and that the hard learned lessons from my experience belonged there. The director of the program was wise beyond her years and was generous with her teachings. With her recommendation, I was hired and began work shortly after my graduation.

Spirit whisper: *This is where you belong and where you can make a difference. Trust in your feelings that tell you that this is the next step in your journey of growth*

I was balancing work, taking care of my children and, at the same time, openly grieving the death of Liam. It was not a walk in the park. Grief is a mysterious thing in that it surprises you every time. At first, there were short periods of time, when I felt that things were easing out; only to be followed by heart wrenching waves of deep grief. The waves hit me when I least expected… I could be in the market and the back of a child's head reminded me of Liam and I would start sobbing… or I would spot a yellow school bus filled with children and remember my son's dream of riding a school bus-- something he did not get to do-- and my heart would break into a myriad pieces…

Spirit whisper: *Know that your child is at peace and take comfort in that knowledge. Humans, because they have bodies, have great difficulty being away from those they love but at the level of spirit, death is another beginning; an opportunity to rest from the struggles that come with being in the body and to take stock on how much spiritual growth has taken place and how much still needs to be learned*

During my first five years at hospice, I took care of adult patients and only covered pediatric patients when the director was on vacation or on leave. I knew that I had to wait until my grief had lessened before I could take care of pediatric patients on a daily basis.

Right after Liam died, I heard, over and over again, from well meaning friends and family members the words: "Time will make things better" and I felt like saying back to them: "You don't know what I am going through. Nothing will take this pain away ever or lessen it". However, after five years, I did feel a slight letting go of the hold grief had over me… I used to relive the last two months of Liam's life: every November, a heavy veil of sadness descended upon my soul and an internal tape would begin to run in my head that made me remember everything that had happened in those last months until he died. After five years, that began to happen in a lesser and lesser measure. The fact that it lessened did not mean that it stopped. It has been almost sixteen years now since Liam's death, and I am still grieving. I will grieve until the moment I take my last breath; this I know but my grief has a deeper understanding now; it is much softer and it does not disrupt my ability to help others.

Spirit whisper: *It is important to heal yourself before you can even attempt to help others*

I have been doing hospice work for the past eleven years and I have found it to be a deeply enriching work which has helped me to continue to grow as a human being as well as a spiritual being. I continue to take care of both adult and pediatric patients and their families and I consider it to be a privilege and an honor to be allowed into their homes and into their hearts.

I have walked the walk of many of the parents of these children as they fight for their child's life, as they advocate for what they feel is best for their child, as they feel wearied because of the well-meaning yet sometimes insensitive comments of relatives and friends, as they feel a fear that is greater than the Universe but cannot talk about it or even allow the feeling into their consciousness… and I am glad to be able to hold their hands, to listen with compassion and understanding, to guide them and support them as they do what they need to do but do not want to do. I have found that…

Spirit whisper: *It is very difficult for children to let go of their loved ones, out of total love for them and of their desire to not hurt them. It is very important to give them permission to let go and to reassure them that the family will be sad but ok; that they will be able to go on*

Chapter Four

TURBULENCE IN
THE CLOUDS...

Winter of 2002-Fall of 2003

While I was taking active steps to find a way to help others with everything I had learned, I was also discovering that I still had a strong desire to connect with a loving man. I began to date a year after the divorce. I found myself feeling completely lost in the dating world because my husband had been my only boyfriend and, needless to say, I was inexperienced. Because I had felt so unloved by my husband, and because I was still actively grieving the death of my son, I was very vulnerable. Basically, I believed everything I was told by men and I had to learn the hard way that words come easily, and that actions speak louder than words.

The first man I became involved with was in his early forties and had been divorced for 5 years. When we met, I was like a desert terrain-- parched and in need of love-- and because of that, his attentions felt like manna to me (heaven sent). Initially, I was blind to the reality of who he was but in time, I began to hear an insistent voice that said...

Spirit whisper: Pay attention. Listen to what he is actually saying and get in touch with how your body responds to his words. Do not discount these messages

After we had dated for eight months, he wanted to take steps towards a serious commitment. I was honest with him when I told him that I didn't know him well enough yet to move forward. He appeared to take it well but his behavior changed after that: he became detached and was distracted when spending time with me. He also stopped inviting me to gatherings with his friends and family. I felt confused by these changes because he denied that there was any problem and said that he wanted to wait until I was ready but he was acting in ways that made me think that the contrary was true. I was not going to rush into something serious until I was absolutely sure and did not appreciate the changes in his behavior. After my failed marriage, I felt I needed to be with someone who could openly tell me what was bothering him and this man, like my ex-husband, was not willing to do that. I did not know what to do. One day, as I sat pondering about this, I clearly heard the following:

Spirit whisper: Why are you feeling so miserable, my child, when you should be feeling happy and ecstatic?

I did not hesitate. I immediately met with him and broke up. I felt a strong sense of peace after I made that decision which confirmed for me the rightness of it.

After that experience, I continued to yearn to share my life with a loving man and felt discouraged by the kind of men I was encountering. So, I decided to spend time working on my own issues as I waited for the right time to meet someone. I told myself that I was busy living a happy life. But the truth is that I was not happy…

During that time, I came across a piece of writing by the poet Peter McWilliams that stayed with me because I felt it expressed very well what I was seeking; it spoke of the importance of spending time to be alone and to let go of the need to be completed by another person. It affirmed my desire to find a kindred spirit who was working on himself, just as I was.

I taped that writing to my bathroom mirror and read it often in order to remind myself of my quest. I continued to grow both as a person and as a professional… I loved working as a hospice social worker and found it to be a perfect fit for the application of the spiritual and life lessons I had gained from my experiences.

Winter of 2005- Winter of 2008

I had signed up for an exercise class at the local gym. The instructor was a thirty-nine year old man, who had been engaged twice before but had never been married and who appeared to be very spiritual. I felt attracted to him but, most of all, I felt flattered by his attentions and by his singling me out during class. One day, I was the only person to show up for class and he took that opportunity to ask me out for tea. I accepted his invitation and as we sat and talked, I asked him: "What matters the most to you in life?" And he responded: "to become a better person each day"… That was my undoing. I immediately put him in the box of someone exactly like me, when it was truly too soon to do that. Words do come easily and are not to be trusted until time has shown them to be true. In his case, they were not true.

After dating for two years, he proposed marriage to me and I accepted. We set a date for one year later. I felt that I knew him because we had spent a lot of time together but it is very easy to pretend to be someone you are not when you are not living with that person. We got married the Fall of 2008 and, a short time later, to my complete and utter shock, he called me on the phone and said to me: "I am tired of pretending"; to which I responded: "Who asked you to pretend? All I have ever asked of you is to be yourself, to show me who you are"… Needless to say I was blindsided; I divorced him as soon as I could and remembered then something that had happened as I had been getting dressed for the wedding… The wedding had taken place at a beautiful flower garden with only us and my children in attendance. As I was dressing, I was alone in the hotel room, when all of the sudden, there was a loud rattling of the mirrored closet doors. I was baffled because there was no reasonable explanation for that to happen: every window and sliding door had been closed at the time. I did not have time to ponder about it then, but I did not forget it…

Spirit whisper: Liam was trying to let you know that you should not get married to this man, in the only way that he could. Spirit sometimes uses light, sounds, smells and objects to get in touch with human beings

I was saddened by this turn of events-- another divorce. However, most of all, I was mad with myself for being taken in; for not seeing the signs. I felt that after years of conscientiously working on myself, to get to know myself and to better myself, how could I have made such a big mistake?

I did not date for years after that experience and, instead, concentrated on my work and on my children who at that time were busy teenagers in need of guidance, mentoring about life, attention and love. But I still desired a loving relationship with a man, and did not want these failed attempts to turn me into an embittered woman who could not see any good in men. I did not want to close my heart to love. My eyes still looked hopefully towards the future to find him.

Spring of 2012- Summer of 2014

I had been living in the Southwest for the past fourteen years and had come to realize that, as a place to live, it was not a good fit for me. To begin with, it was not cold enough. I longed for snowy winters and more clearly defined seasons.

A year after my daughter went off to college, I decided to move to a beautiful city which suited me to perfection. I had not dated anyone for four years and was very content being with myself (or so I thought). However, from time to time, I would say to myself: "If a good man crosses my path, I am open to getting to know him." I realize now that some part of me still yearned to share my life with a man. I was not aware of the yearning; I had buried it deep inside of me and was not in touch with it. Because of not being aware, I was not prepared for what happened next…

A few months after the move, in the Spring of 2012, I met a man who surprised me by the pull I felt in his presence. He was in his late forties and I was unaware of how he used his eyes in order to rope me in. He was used to doing this and he was very good at it. Like I said before, being unaware of the fact that I was lying to myself as to what my needs were, rendered me very vulnerable to this particular person. He appeared to give me his undivided attention and to be very caring and educated but the reality of it was that he wanted to appear that way. He was a very good actor…

I fell for his act - hook, line and sinker. When I found out that he had been divorced three times, I pushed aside any red flags about that fact and chose to believe that he, like me, had difficulty in choosing well when it came to partners. When he told me that he was serious about me; I chose to believe that he saw the potential of sharing a future with me. When after a year, he did not mention anything close to imagining us together long-term, I began to doubt his sincerity and his intentions. However, I was under a spell and a strong one…

In time, his act began to fray at the edges… When he would get angry about not getting his way, or choose to vent his anger at me because of all the choices he was not making in his life, I began to see a different side of him; I started to realize that our motivations in life were vastly different which made it impossible for me to imagine a future with him.

Spirit whisper: *From the beginning, I have sent you messages about this man; every time you have felt uneasy and confused by his words and/or behavior, I was letting you know that he was not trustworthy. Do not disregard the inklings, the reactions of your body to what a person says or does, because in those "gut feelings" lie encapsulated all the wisdom you need to make the right choices about your life and about your relationships*

When I broke things off with this man, I was at peace. I knew deep inside that the mistake was all mine. The anger I felt was not towards him: he did not wish to grow; he was doing what he had been doing all his life: putting on a good act… However, I, on the other hand, had been intent on growing, on seeing reality as it is; had been committed to the truth, not only with myself but also with seeing the truth in others, and I had failed catastrophically with him.

I saw then that the same truth kept presenting itself to me and that I kept refusing to see it; until, finally, finally, finally, I chose to see myself as I was and consciously chose to let go of any attachment to the idea that I needed to share my life with a man in order to be happy… and that decision, that realization, changed everything for me.

Chapter Five

PEACEFUL QUIETUDE...

Summer of 2015

It has been over a year since the breakup of my last romantic relationship and I have to thank that person for leading me to the final stage of my realization about romantic relationships. I have no desire now to share my life with someone; I finally feel full and complete all on my own and I see that all these years I thought I was searching for someone to share my life with… what I was actually searching for was myself, my own self-love, my own completion. And I am finally there… Thanks to all those who came before him, to all the men who taught me to not seek fulfillment in them, but only within myself. What a gift!

Nowadays, I have changed the writing on my bathroom mirror to:

Love is… Loving oneself; Seeing reality with eyes wide open

Letting go of the need to be with another person; Feeling perfectly at peace

Sharing this beautiful world with humanity; Reveling in living in the moment

And feeling deeply grateful for this sacred opportunity to grow spiritually

My life now is much different than it was nineteen years ago, before the storm hit; I live simply and peacefully, engaging in activities that bring me joy and earning a living doing meaningful and beautiful work. This does not mean that my life is perfect; there is still so much that I have to learn! I continue to work diligently on shedding my fears, on maintaining a healthy balance in all areas of my life, on growing in forgiveness and wisdom. I have periods when I am closer to feeling balanced than others but working towards this is well worth the effort. Most importantly, my energy is not directed towards meeting someone to share my life with because when I was doing that, I was not believing that I could be happy by myself, that I could take care of myself and I was not trusting in God and the Universe to be with me and to provide for my every need. I have finally discarded the cloak of deeply assimilated societal messages that kept me thinking limited thoughts and believing in limiting beliefs about life and about my potential. I feel that the possibilities open to me at this point in my life are truly limitless…

Chapter Six

A COSMIC SHOWER OF GIFTS

THE GIFTS...

The first gift: Letting go of the fear of dying

Why am I so afraid of dying?

The second gift: Trust in your intuition

Why does my mind discount my gut feelings?

The third gift: Clarity of vision

Who am I and what am I here in this world for?

The fourth gift: Awareness of ephemerality of the human existence

How can we live while knowing that we can die at any moment?

The fifth gift: A wider perspective

Why do children die?

The sixth gift: Letting go of control of your life and the lives of others

How can we stop worrying that something bad

can happen to ourselves or to our children?

The seventh gift: Conditional versus Unconditional love

What is love?

When I think of Liam, I see a beautiful being who, just like a shooting star, shone brightly for a brief moment leaving behind a beautiful sparkling trail. My heart expands when, in my mind's eye, I see his twinkling green eyes, full of mischief, or hear his sweet voice always asking about something, with such an insatiable curiosity about life… as if he knew that time was of the essence. But most of all, when I think of him, I feel the immensity of the love he showered all he loved with; even after death, visiting me in dreams, giving me hugs and reassuring me of his love. I am so deeply grateful for the hand he had in the personal transformation I continue to go through while on this beautiful planet…

The **first gift** was the realization that letting go of fears allows us to live life more fully. In the fall of 1994, I boarded a plane, to New Zealand, with Liam and Ethan; after strapping them in their seats, I got in touch with how afraid I was feeling … and I remember Liam, six years old, holding my hand and infusing me with peace during the whole flight. He was always such a teacher, even before the storm started… After his death, I came to terms with the realization that I was no longer afraid of dying; that I was looking forward to the moment when I would be reunited with my son.

Why am I so afraid of dying?

Spirit whisper: There is nothing to fear because you are being taken care of. To live in fear of death is not to live. Random events can happen at any time; trust that no matter what happens all will be well. Death is not the worst thing that can happen; the worst thing is a life not "lived"; a life spent worrying about the future or the past or death; a life where minimal spiritual growth takes place

The **second gift** was that I began to trust in my intuition. I feel that spirit had been whispering to me all my life but I had discounted the validity of those whispers, until after Liam's illness. This could not have been more obvious to me than in the area of relationships. There were so many instances when I received a message about someone I was dating: crystal clear-- a message that informed me that the person was not trustworthy, that he was lying and I just did not want to hear it; my need to be with someone was too strong so I would push the whispers aside and, eventually, had to learn the hard way that I had been wrong. It took such a jolt in my life to make me begin to listen and it took many years after that for me to come to trust in the spirit guidance that is available to all of us-- if only we are open to it.

Why does my mind discount my gut feelings?

$\mathcal{S}$pirit whisper: *All human beings have an inner compass that informs them as to whether their thoughts and actions make them feel good or bad. This is their conscience. In addition to that, they retain a connection, a chord if you will, to the spiritual world that can offer guidance in navigating the seemingly uncertain waters of this earthly existence. However, more often than not, human beings ignore this guidance. They do so mainly because, unless they have proof of where this guidance comes from, they cannot believe in it. Human beings have become dependent on their brain and its mental activities to the point of excluding other ways of receiving valuable information and guidance. As they increase in their ability to question the status quo, in their selectivity as to what is being fed to them from outside sources and in their self-awareness, their ability to open themselves up to the wisdom of the universe through their intuition will increase exponentially*

The **third gift** was the clarity of vision as to what we come into this world for and the fact that it is imperative that we make our existence count. Without realizing it, I had not been living my life; I had been letting life "live" me. I had been on automatic pilot: taking care of my children, trying to figure out what was not working in my marriage, spending my time on superficial matters in order to try to fill an existential void I had inside of me. Basically, I was merely surviving… I was deeply unhappy and was not taking time to reflect, to get in touch with myself. All that changed, after Liam's illness and subsequent death… I realized then that there is no time for pettiness, for pretending to be someone you are not, for giving your energy to anything that does not make you feel good as a person or does not fulfill you. As a result, I went back to school and found my personal calling as a hospice social worker. The clarity I received to see what truly matters in the world freed me to let go of things that used to worry me or cause me discomfort. I realized that one cannot live worrying about what others think of you. I used to care about such things. I suffered significantly in the past from the inability of others to accept me as I was or their insensitivity towards what I was going through.

I was a people pleaser and felt joy from giving my love to others without realizing that I was expecting love in return. However, there is nothing more effective as being hit by the bolt of lightning of your child being terminally ill and dying to make it clear to you that what matters is to behave from a solid center of integrity, truth and good will in all you do and that if somebody does not like it, then, that is their right.

Who am I and what am I here in this world for?

Spirit whisper: The human experience on earth is just a blip in time and to keep this in mind can help human beings to let go of anything that can distract them from what truly matters: their progress towards greater spiritual growth and awareness. When people are in the body, it can be as if people are in a heavy fog which makes it almost impossible to see clearly where they are going or where they need to go. Because of this, it is hard to figure out even who they are so they begin to accumulate the feedback that others give them and to utilize it to construct an idea of who they are. And if the feedback is good, that makes them feel worthy and good about themselves, so they begin to need to be on the good side of others and so a cycle of needing to be liked and approved of by others begins. Conversely, if the feedback is bad, an even greater need to receive approval is born. As people open up their eyes to the truths of life, they can begin to shed their need for approval and can become empowered by their own knowledge of who they are, what they are here on this earth to do and what matters in this life

The **fourth gift** was that I became keenly aware that our loved ones can be gone at any time so we had better show them how much they mean to us at every opportunity we can. Whereas before I would nonchalantly say goodbye to my loved ones as they left to run an errand, or go to school; that was no longer possible for me after Liam's death. To this day, every time I part from my loved ones, I feel compelled to hug them tightly and to tell them I love them because I know first-hand that their return is not guaranteed and that I need to take any and every chance to profess my love and appreciation to them. Even though, this may sound morbid, it does not feel that way. Living in a death-denying society where we seem to be obsessed with staying young and death is still a taboo subject, it is even more imperative to face death squarely in the face in order to befriend it; in order to feel a softness come over us; in order to act and live from a profound sense of love. I no longer take for granted that my children will outlive me; I no longer take for granted that I will be here tomorrow. I simply make every effort to remind myself to enjoy today and everyday fully…

How can we live while knowing that we can die at any moment?

Spirit whisper: *The universe is vast and consists of an immensely loving force. Death is neither a bad thing nor a good thing. It just is. It can happen at any time and there is not very much anyone can do about it. The best thing to do is to make every moment count and to remain aware of the ephemeral quality of existence. Since people are spiritual beings in human bodies, of course, they are going to grieve the death of loved ones; then, keeping in mind that at any given moment death can greet them or their loved ones, will allow them to have the sharper focus necessary to induce them to express loving feelings and gratitude to everyone they know and love and to do so at every opportunity they can*

The **fifth** gift was the development of a wider perspective as to why things like these happen to children. As a result of my experience with Liam, I realized that we make pacts with our children and they make pacts with us while we are still spirits, before we enter our earthly bodies: pacts as to how we hope to help each other grow spiritually during our lifetime together. And this realization fills me with immense gratitude and admiration for this child whose spirit agreed to go through a terminal illness in order to help those around him open their eyes to a higher perspective and grow in their capacity to give love to others. I am a better mother to Ethan and Noelle because of the awareness through Liam, that the love our children give us is completely unconditional and that we need to treasure it. Their love is as pure as we imagine heaven to be.

Why do children die?

$\mathcal{S}$pirit whisper: *The reason spirits come to be in an earthly body is in order to grow spiritually. Liam chose his parents, brother and sister and chose to go in a painful journey of experiencing a terminal illness as a child with the purpose to not only grow spiritually himself but also to jolt his family awake into the realization that all that matters is the quality of your love. It is not your riches, it is not your power, it is not your fame, it is not your work… It is only how well you have loved-- yourself, your loved ones, and the world-- that matters ultimately. And in order to deeply assimilate this truth, you have to be able to know what unconditional love feels like and you have to be able to shed the wrong messages you have received from others about love. Look only to your children and you will know how it feels to be loved in this way…*

The **sixth gift** was the loosening up of the control I felt I had in life. Before the storm happened, I had been constantly afraid for my children; I thought: "If something happens to me, who will take care of them?" However, after all was said and done, I felt deep in the marrow of my bones, that that was no way to live.

Around that time, I came across a book by Kahlil Gibran entitled "The Prophet" and in it, his writing "On Children" deeply resonated with my new way of seeing life. In a very spiritual way, he talks about the fact that our children are not ours, even though that is what we humans think and believe; they belong to the Universe.

I stopped worrying so much about my children and started allowing myself to float in the river of life and to follow wherever its currents led me, knowing that a wise presence was guiding me.

How can we stop worrying that something bad can happen to ourselves or our children?

Spirit whisper: *When spirits enter the body realm, they forget their true selves. During infancy and early childhood, they still remember who they are and act from that knowledge. They completely trust in their parents to take care of their every need and they do not worry. As they grow, they begin to forget, aided by the parental and societal teachings which can instill fear, separation and feelings of inadequacy in them. Most parents spend many hours fretting over their children and their well being; however, getting in touch with the perfection of the Universe, of all that is, can lead them to take a deep breath, to relax into existence and to trust in the unknown. It is imperative that adults realize that part of growing spiritually involves returning to the trust, joy and present moment awareness they had as children but with the added wisdom that comes with experience and age*

The **seventh gift** and the most important gift of all was the realization at a deeper level that love is an unconditional force and that being able to differentiate between how conditional versus unconditional love feels is crucial. I also realized that romantic love is limited and is not to be mistaken for true love. I experienced true love for the first time as a force coming from my firstborn, Liam, and I continue to feel it to this day from Ethan and Noelle.

Up until the storm, I had taken the love my parents, family, friends and husband gave me as the role model for love. I did not realize that their love was conditional... My parents loved me if... I was a good girl; if... I lived life according to their vision; if... I behaved the way they approved of; if... As a result, I also loved conditionally and took that to be what love is. And even though I had had three children when Liam became ill, I still was not in touch with the quality of the love they (my children) were giving me because I was still too immersed in my own miserable feelings of sadness-- due to my disappointing and empty marriage. It was only after the onset of my son's illness that I began to pay attention to him and began to feel that the quality of his love was different and in extension, the quality of the love Ethan and Noelle offered to me was different as well. Their love was unconditional, it did not ask anything of me other than for me to be around them, it forgave me instantly any faults and it was warm and pure like no other love I have ever experienced.

What is love?

Spirit whisper: *Currently, the world has an imbalance. Human beings are spending an immense amount of time and energy trying to find a partner in order to feel complete and in order to not be alone. They have acquired the habit of wanting to have someone with them and are keeping very busy in order to avoid thinking; in order to escape the stresses of everyday life. However, it is essential for humans to become comfortable with their own aloneness-- in order to be able to take the time to look within and to heal the emotional wounds that they have been carrying. This is important because the more unhealed wounds a person has, the more conditional the love they offer to themselves and to others is.*

Romantic love is a fallacy. Nobody can complete someone else because humans must complete themselves. In fact, it is imperative for them to do so, if they wish to grow spiritually. In order to accomplish this, they need to let go of the deeply entrenched messages that they have assimilated while growing up; messages that keep them spinning their wheels in search for completion outside of themselves. And the best example to follow is that of young children. It could be said that the Universe breathes pure love and that children are the sacred deliverers of this love to all human beings. Children are not searching for someone to complete them, nor are they worrying about who is going to provide for them… They know they are fine the way they are. Young children see the best in their parents, forgive and forget easily, live in the present and are open to pure joy. By paying close attention to the quality of the love children offer to them, human beings can begin to transform themselves, to go within in order to find out who they are and to become authentic and transparent. And this, in turn, will allow them to let go of the need to receive security and completion from other human beings and to take the leap into trusting in God and the Universe to provide for their every need, to guide them in their journey of self-awareness and to put the right people in their paths to help them grow. In doing this, profound healing will take place and the quality of the love they offer will change from conditional to unconditional. And when humans heal themselves, when they heal their accumulated wounds, they begin to extend love towards themselves and the more love they feel for themselves, the more love they will be able to extend to others. They will become softer, less judgmental, less hard on themselves, less uptight... This will lead them to commit themselves to being truthful and to being good to their bodies and minds and to offer respect to themselves; in time, they will come to see that what matters is that they are doing the best they can at any given moment and that so is everyone else.

Even though, human beings believe that there are many kinds of love, the truth is that there is only one love: unconditional love. Whether it is extended to a child, a parent, a friend, a stranger, a partner, an animal, a rock or a tree... It is only love if it is unconditional and in order to reach that point, humans must have healed themselves enough to be able to offer unconditional love to themselves first.

Only from healed hearts can unconditional love spring forth...

Author's note

I began this journey eighteen years ago as a deeply unhappy woman who spent most of her time trying to make sense of how her life had not turned out they way she had envisioned, and who ignored the voice of Spirit

The unexpected thunderbolt of my son's diagnosis and subsequent death served as the catalyst for the beginning of a deeply personal and spiritual transformation…

My journey continues but I am a different woman now; a woman who listens and trusts in the voice of Spirit and who, out of her sad loss, has made it through a dark tunnel and is now walking in the bright light that comes with the deepest of all realizations: that it is important to become aware of what love is… A benevolent force which stems from self-love and radiates outwards to all areas of our lives; nurturing and enriching us and all those in its vicinity

To The Reader

May you hear the subtle yet persistent nudgings of Spirit in your life
and may you experience the peace that only unconditional love can bring

ABOUT THE AUTHOR

Camila Abbot has worked as a hospice social worker for the past eleven years. Eighteen years ago, she had a life-changing experience, which she is choosing to share with the world in this book, her first literary effort. You can find her on Facebook for discussion and inspiration. She lives in Michigan's Upper Peninsula.

Printed in the United States
By Bookmasters